Dea

Proud

Isabel Thomas

Illustrated by Clare Elsom

Raintree

Raintree is an imprint of Capstone Global Library Limited, a company incorporated in England and Wales having its registered office at 7 Pilgrim Street, London, EC4V 6LB – Registered company number: 6695582

www.raintreepublishers.co.uk
myorders@raintreepublishers.co.uk

Edited by Dan Nunn, Rebecca Rissman, and Catherine Veitch
Designed by Philippa Jenkins
Original illustrations © Clare Elsom
Illustrated by Clare Elsom
Production by Victoria Fitzgerald
Originated by Capstone Global Library Ltd
Printed and bound in China

ISBN 978 1 406 25042 8 (hardback)
16 15 14 13 12
10 9 8 7 6 5 4 3 2 1

ISBN 978 1 406 25052 7 (paperback)
17 16 15 14
10 9 8 7 6 5 4 3 2 1

British Library Cataloguing in Publication Data
Thomas, Isabel.
Proud. -- (Dealing with Feeling...)
155.2-dc23
A full catalogue record for this book is available from the British Library.

Contents

Some words are shown in bold, **like this.** Find
out what they mean in the glossary on page 23.

What is pride?

happy

caring

jealous

sad

Pride is a **feeling**. It is normal to have many kinds of feelings every day.

Some feelings are nice to have. Pride is a nice feeling. We feel proud when we are pleased with ourselves.

What makes people feel proud?

When somebody says that we are
kind or look good, we feel proud.
It is nice to get a **compliment**.

We feel proud when we do something well or achieve a goal. We feel proud when we are brave and do something that scares us.

What does pride feel like?

When you are proud, you feel good about yourself.

You might feel more **confident.**
Pride can make you want to work
hard and do well again.

How can pride make other people feel?

People show their **feelings** in different ways. Feeling proud can make us act like we are more important than other people.

It might look as if we are **showing off**. This can make other people feel jealous, angry, or sad.

What if other people do not seem pleased for me?

It is normal to feel proud when you do something well. It can be hard when other people do not seem pleased for you.

Remember that they have **feelings**, too. They might feel sad that they are not the best this time.

How should I deal with pride?

Sometimes we feel proud because we have something that other people **admire**. It is nice to feel proud. It is not nice to **boast** about what you have.

When you feel proud, remember not to **show off**. You can be a good friend by sharing what you have.

What if I have nothing to be proud about?

Everyone has something to feel proud about. Ask your friends why they like spending time with you.

Ask your family what they like most about you. You can be proud of being a great brother or sister, a great son or daughter, or a great friend.

What can I do to feel proud?

You can feel proud by working hard at school. You can feel proud when you help out at home.

18

You do not have to BE the best to
be proud of yourself. You just have
to DO your best.

How can I help other people to feel proud?

You can make people feel proud by giving them **compliments**. It is nice to make other people feel good about themselves.

If you are good at doing something, try teaching other people how to do it. Everyone feels proud when they learn something new.

Make a pride toolbox

Write down some tips to help you feel proud every day.

Talk about how you have helped other people.

Think about how you help out around your home.

What things are you good at in school?

Keep a note of praise you get at school and at home.

List some new skills that you have learned.

Remember nice things people have said about you.

Think of what makes you a good friend.

Think of times that you have been brave.

Glossary

admire think that something is good

boast talk about things that you have or can do in a way that makes other people feel bad

compliment when you tell somebody something that you like about them

confident feeling that you can do something well

feeling something that happens inside our minds. It can affect our bodies and the way we behave.

show off boast about things that you have or can do

Find out more

Books

All Kinds of Feelings: A Lift-the-Flap Book,
 Emma Brownjohn (Tango Books, 2003)

Glad Monster, Sad Monster: A Book About
 Feelings, Ed Emberley and Anne Miranda
 (Little, Brown, 1997)

Websites

bbc.co.uk/scotland/education/health/feelings

kidshealth.org/kid/feeling

pbskids.org/arthur/games/aboutface

Index